Pipe-Majo[r]

W. ROSS'S

COLLECTION

OF

HIGHLAND
BAGPIPE
MUSIC

BOOK 1

All tunes in this Book are arranged by
Pipe-Major W. Ross and are copyright.

PATERSON'S PUBLICATIONS

LONDON, ENGLAND

CONTENTS.

The Abercairney Highlanders. March.

2

The Edinburgh Volunteers. March.

The Glengarry Gathering. March.

Angus MacKay.

6 Captain P. D. Wallace.   March.   W. Ross.

Cameronian Rant.

Reel.

Leaving Glendale. March. By D. A. Campbell.

Captain Norman Orr Ewing.   March.   W. Ross.

10

Mrs. H. L. Macdonald of Dunach.   March.

By W. Lawrie.

Pretty Lilian.   March.   By George Mackay (Edinburgh.)

Kantara to El. Arish.

March.

By Pipe Major W Fergusson.

Brigadier General. Ronald Cheape of Tiroran.   March.

W. Ross.

The Hills of South Uist.

March.

By Pipe Major J. Steel.

Craig-n-darroch.　　　　　March

Bonnie Ann.

March.

18 THE BRAEMAR HIGHLANDERS   March

Mrs. Hugh Calder.

March.

By Rod. Campbell.

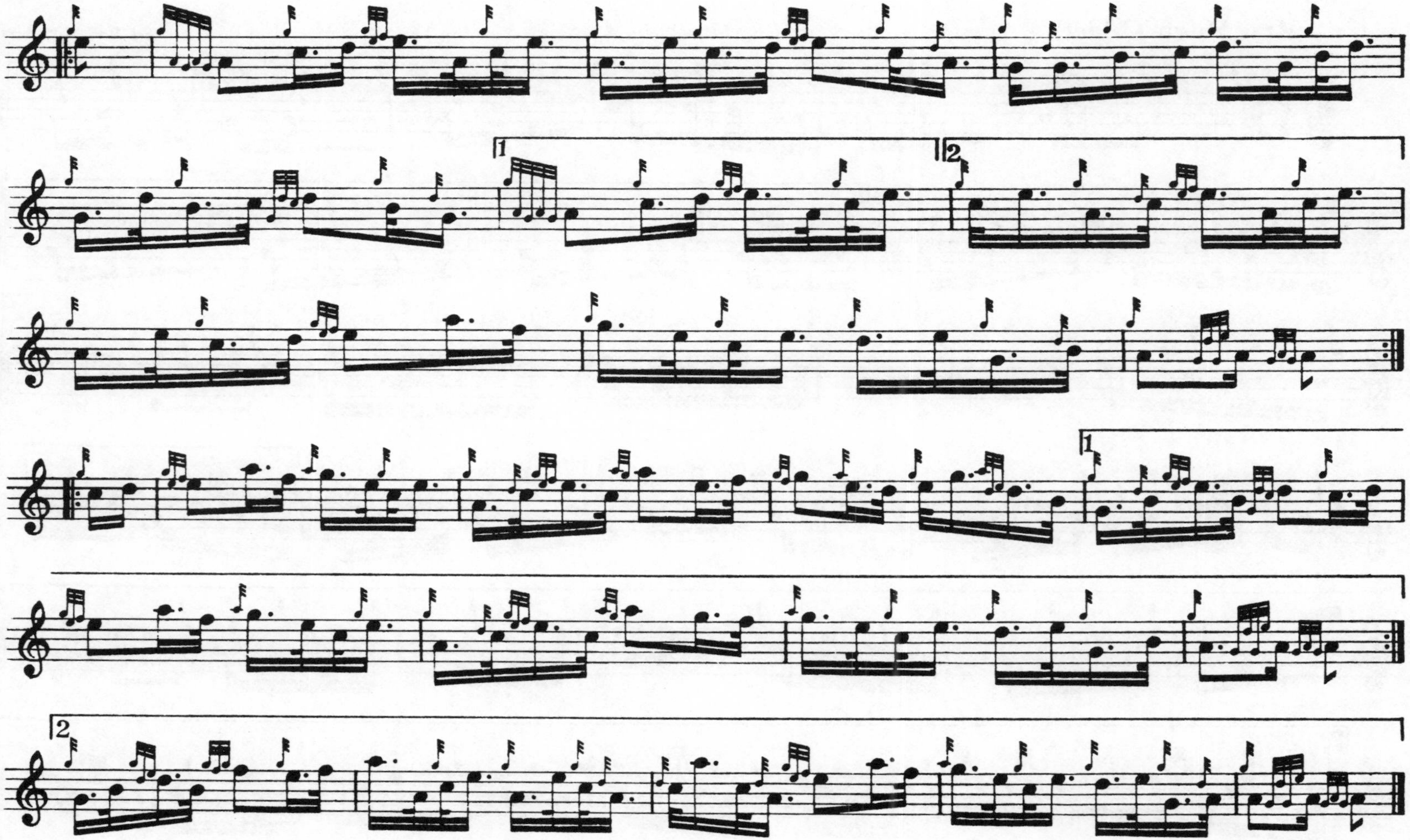
1
2
1
2

CHARLES EDWARD HOPE VERE

March

H. MacKay

The Highland Wedding.　　　　March.

Ian MacLeod. Slow March. Geo. MacKay.

Charlie's Welcome. Reel.

Ca' the Ewes.   Reel.

The Rejected Suitor. Reel.

28

The Flaggon.   Reel.

MacAlister's Dirk. Reel.

John MacKechnie.

Reel.

Bridge of Perth.　　　　　　**Reel.**

The Eight Men of Moidart. Reel.

Struy Lodge. Reel. W. Ross.

33

Jacky Latin   Reel.

Willie Gray.　　　　　　　　　　　Strathspey.

South Uist Golf Club.　　　　　　　Strathspey.　　　　　　　L. Mac Cormick

Athole Cummers.   **Strathspey.**

The Piper's Bonnet.

The Pipers Bonnet.

Strathspey.

Blair Drummond.   Strathspey.

Delvin Side.　　　　　　　　　　　Strathspey.

Tulloch Gorm. Strathspey.

Cannich, Bridge. Jig.

Malcolm, MacPhersons. Jig.

The Baldooser.

Jig.

3rd & 4th Parts added by W. Ross.

The Shaggy Grey Buck.

Jig

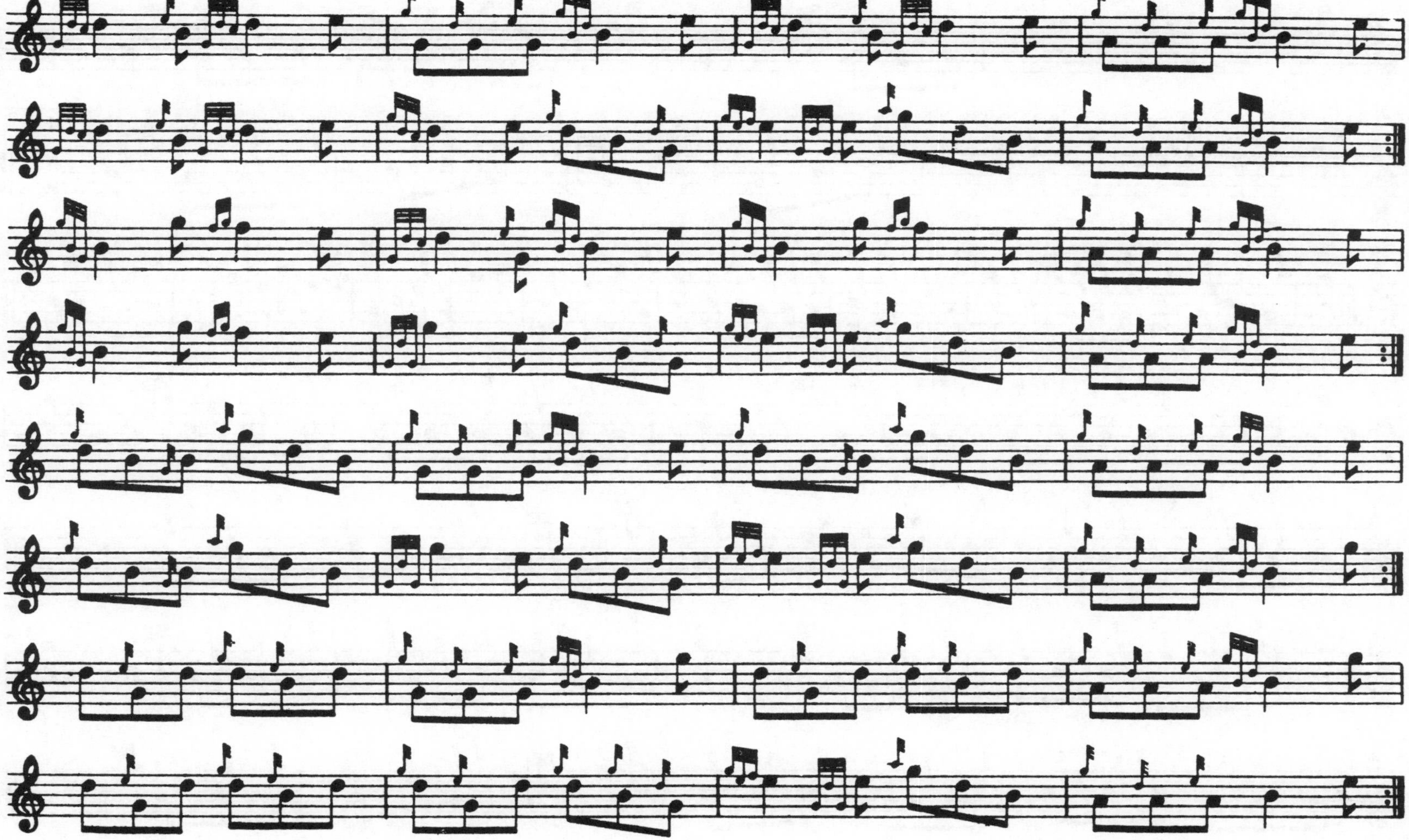

Miss Proud.   Reel.

Pretty Marion.   **Reel.**

50

Captain Jack Murray.   Strathspey.

Hugh Calder.   Strathspey.   By Rod Campbell.

THE STIRLINGSHIRE MILITIA

March

H. MacKay

Brigadier General Lorne Campbell, V.C. of Akarit.　March.

by Angus McPherson
Inveran 1943

1st Time

2nd Time

1st Time

2nd Time

Angus Campbells. Farewell to Stirling. March.

Printed by Caligraving Limited Thetford Norfolk England

9/95 (22492)